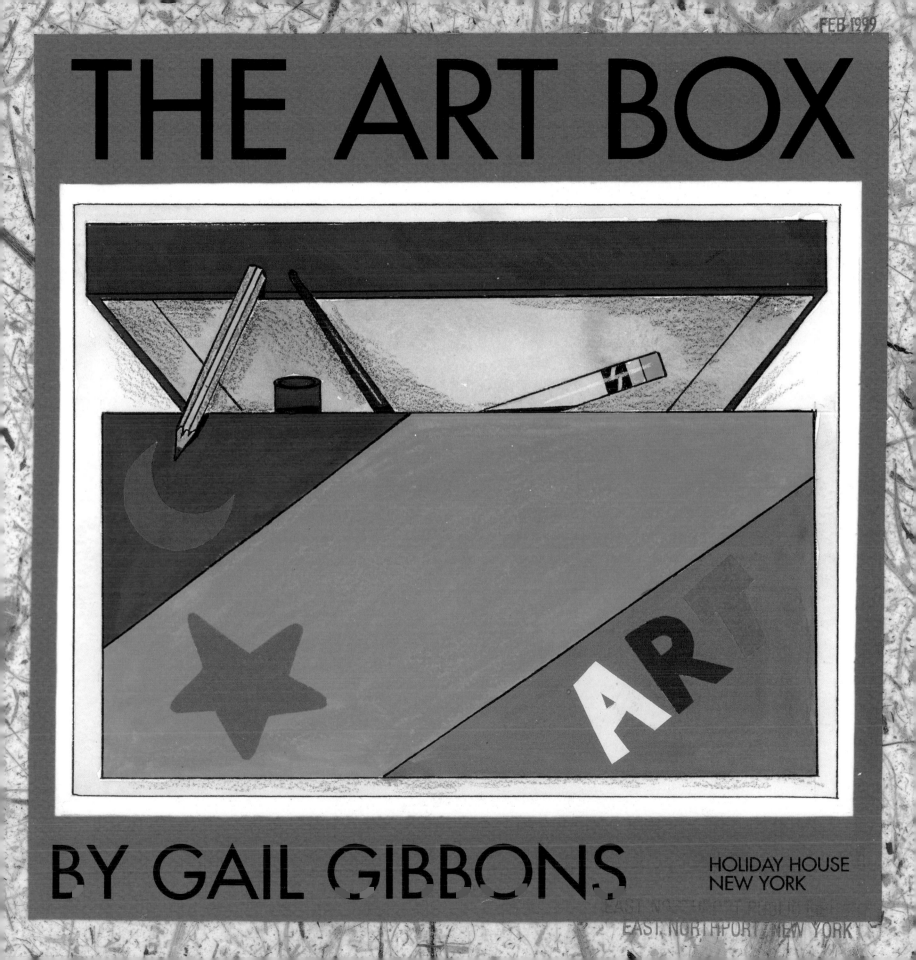

THE ART BOX

BY GAIL GIBBONS

HOLIDAY HOUSE
NEW YORK

FOR MARILEE OLANDER

Library of Congress Cataloging-in-Publication Data
Gibbons, Gail.
    The art box / written and illustrated by Gail Gibbons. — 1st ed.
        p.   cm.
    Summary: Describes the many different kinds of tools and supplies
which artists use to produce their work.
    ISBN 0-8234-1386-1
    1. Artists' materials—Juvenile literature.   2. Artists' tools—
Juvenile literature.   [1. Artists' materials.]   I. Title.
N8530.G53   1998   97-44171   CIP   AC
702'.8—dc21

Special thanks to Harry Pearson of
Duke's Art and Frame Shop,
Hanover, New Hampshire

Out of the art box come...

PENCILS

CHALKS

COLORED CHALK

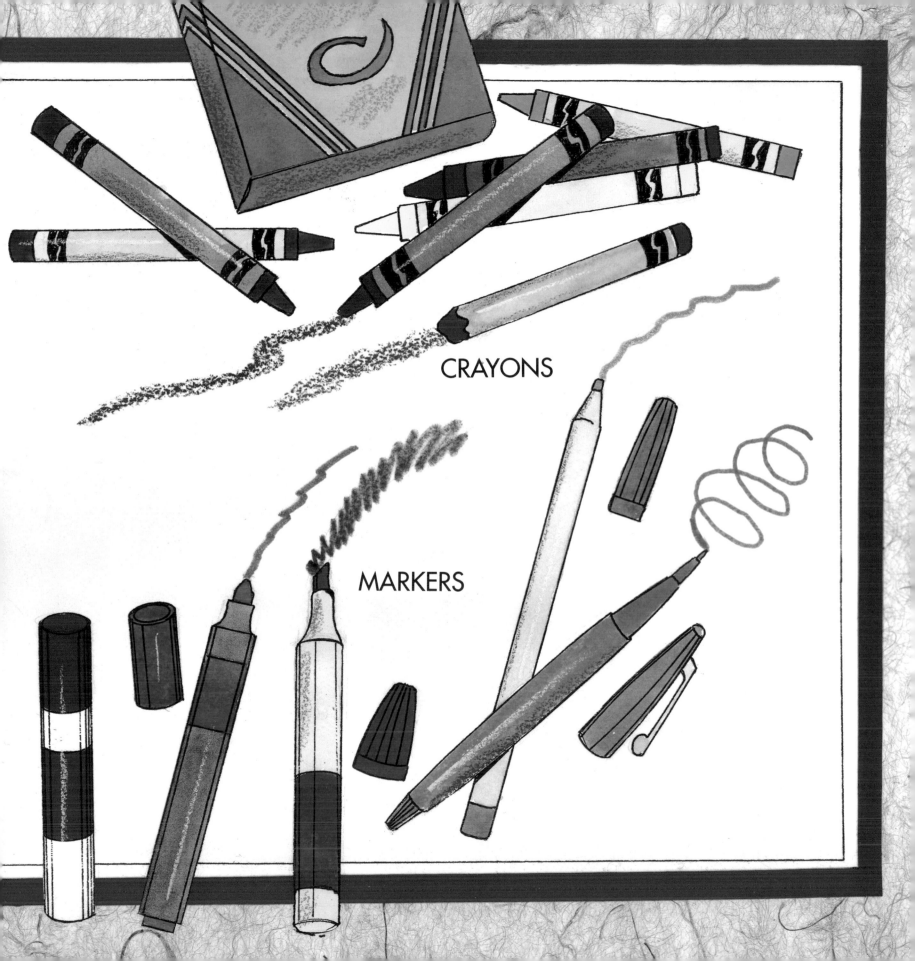

CRAYONS

MARKERS

PENS AND INKS

COLORED PENCILS

All of these are used to draw.

Next to the art box are...

MANY KINDS OF PAPER

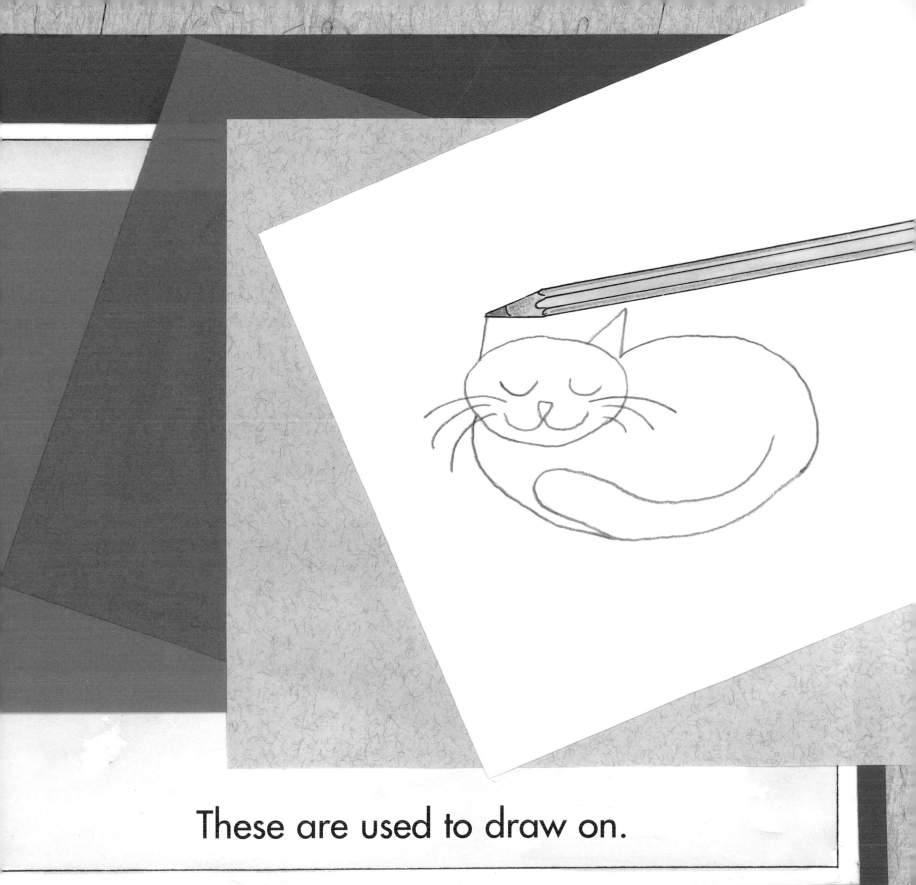

These are used to draw on.

Out of the art box come....

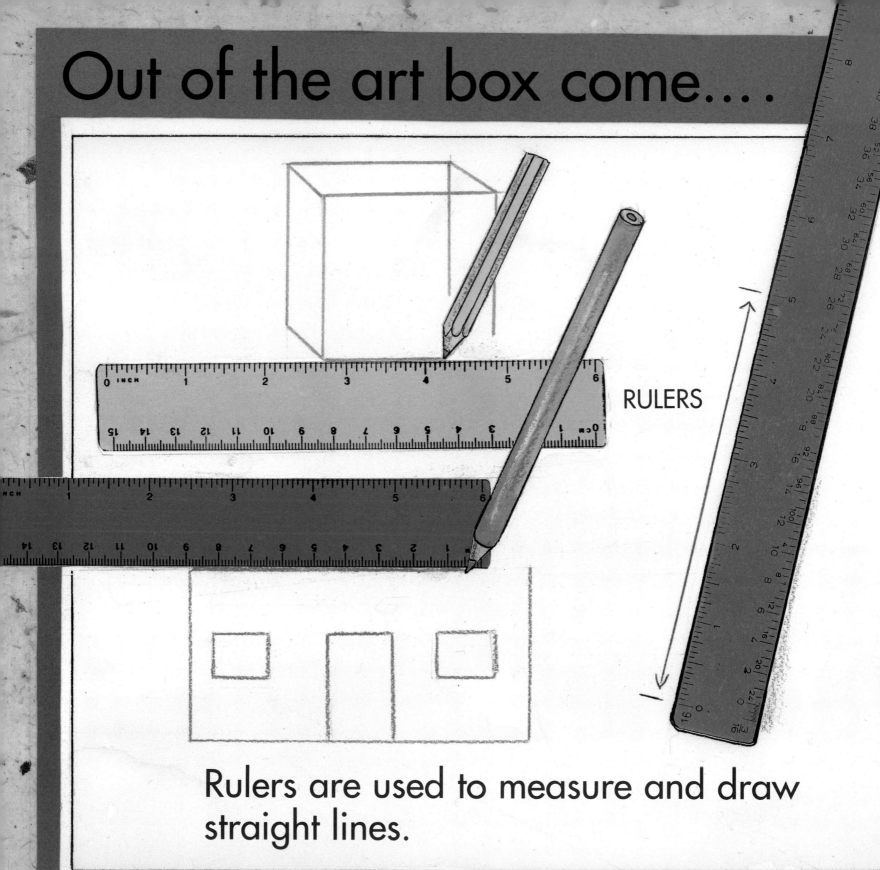

RULERS

Rulers are used to measure and draw straight lines.

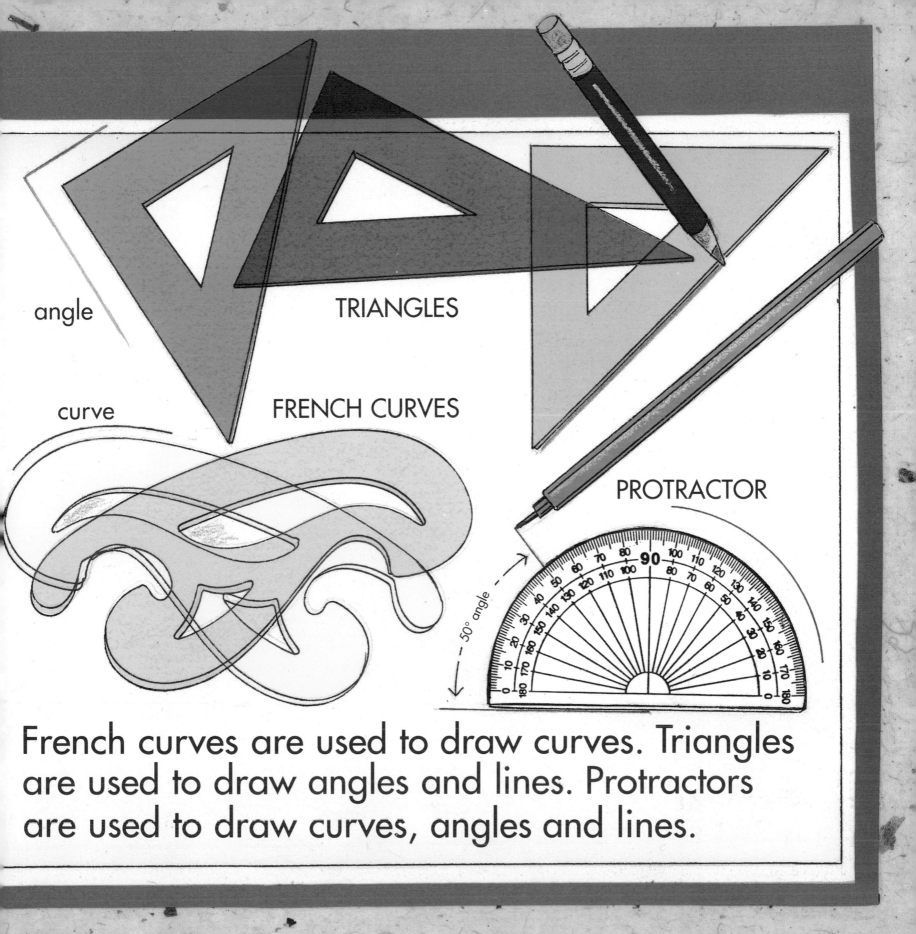

angle

curve

TRIANGLES

FRENCH CURVES

PROTRACTOR

50° angle

French curves are used to draw curves. Triangles are used to draw angles and lines. Protractors are used to draw curves, angles and lines.

CIRCLE GUIDE

PENCIL SHARPENER

COMPASS

Circle guides and a compass are used to draw curves and circles. A pencil sharpener makes a pencil point sharp.

OOPS...

ERASERS

Erasers can remove what you don't want.

TAPE

PASTE

GLUE

Tape, paste, and glue hold pieces of paper or other things in place.

SCISSORS

Scissors may be used to cut paper.

Out of the art box come...

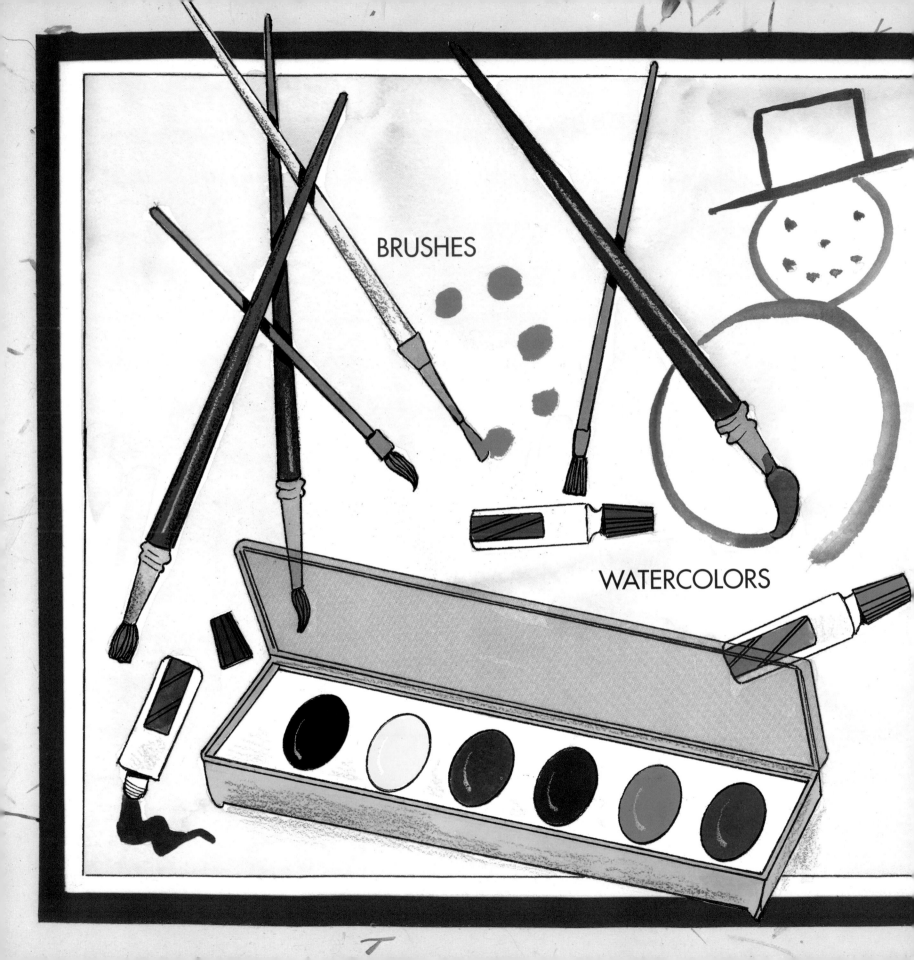

BRUSHES

WATERCOLORS

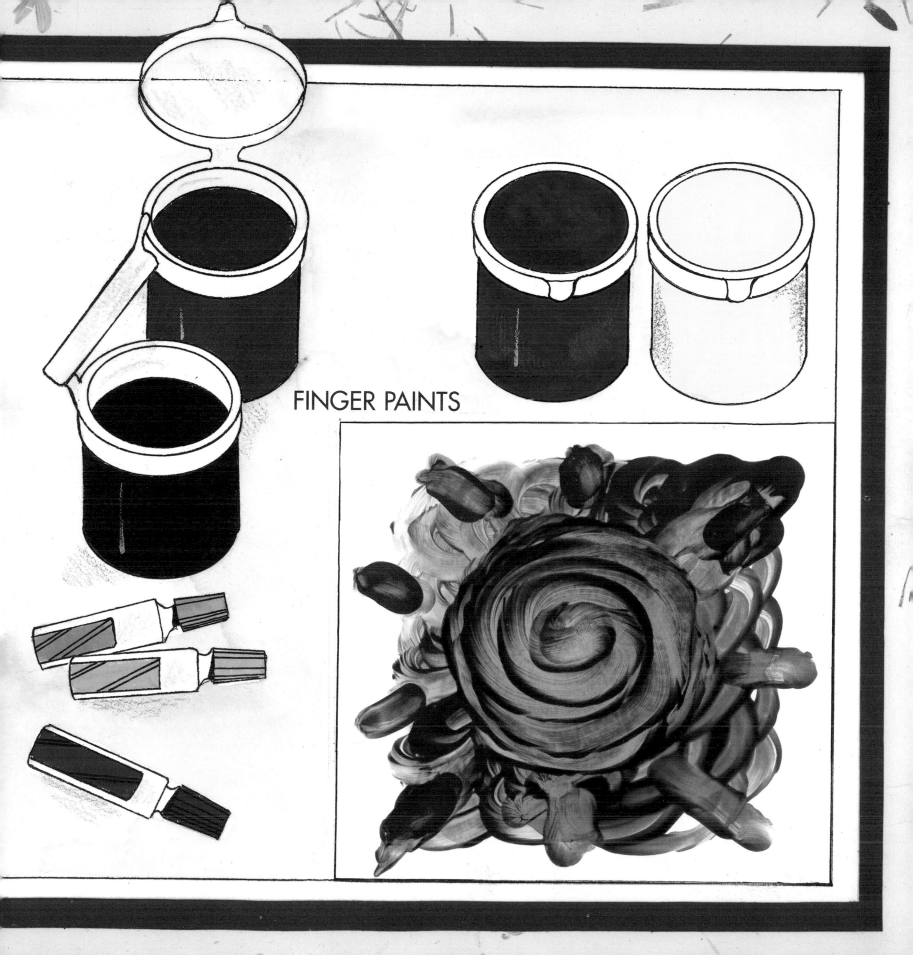

FINGER PAINTS

TEMPERA PAINTS, also called POSTER PAINTS

ACRYLIC PAINTS

OIL PAINTS

All of these are used for painting.

Next to the art box are...

PAPERS

CANVASES

These are used to paint on.

PALETTE

EASEL

thumbhole

Easels can hold a canvas or a big pad of
paper. A palette is used to hold paints and
to mix different colors.

These three colors are called the PRIMARY COLORS.

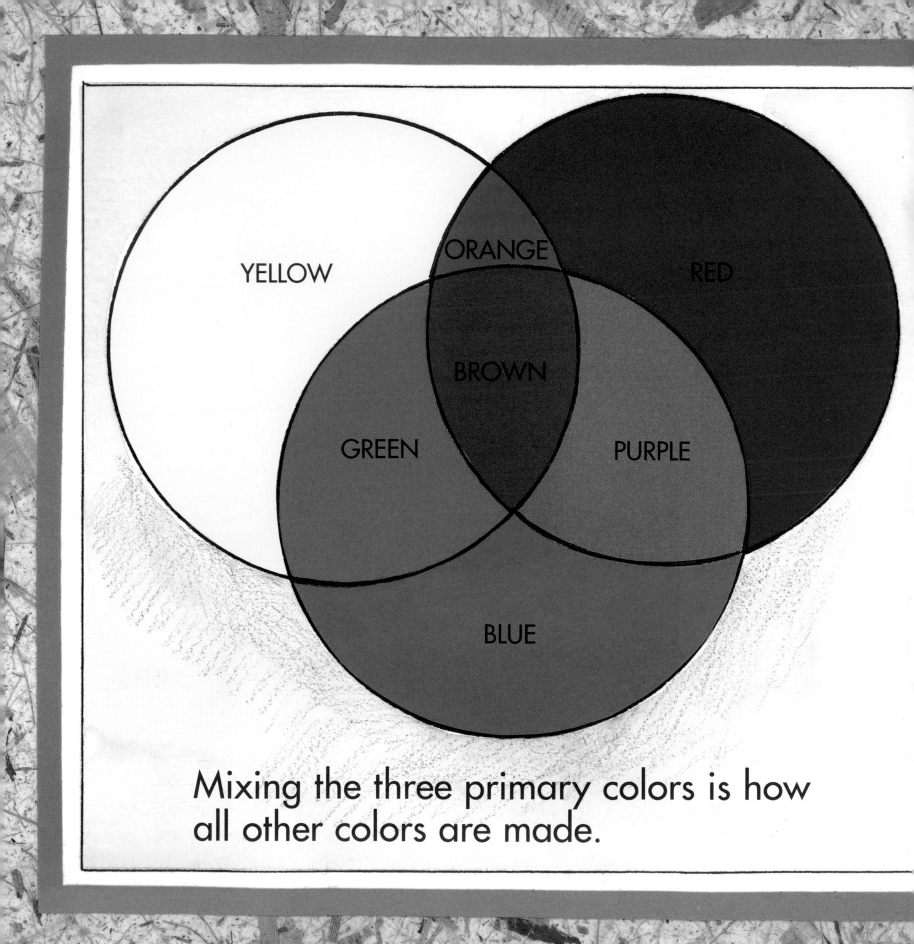

Mixing the three primary colors is how all other colors are made.

WHITE

GRAY

BLACK

Black is used to darken a color. White lightens a color.

COLORS . . .

Artists can express themselves when
they draw or paint.

Out of an artist's imagination

You can collect supplies to fill your own
art box.

$16.95

DATE			

FEB 1999

BAKER & TAYLOR